Max and Jake

Story by Joan Jarden
Illustrations by Richard Hoit

Max went to play
with his new friend, Jake.

"Hello, Max," said Jake.
"Mom is taking me
to the swimming pool today.
Do you want to come with us?"

"I can't swim," said Max.

"I can help you," said Jake.
"I'm good at swimming."

"Can Grandpa come with us?"
said Max.

"Yes," smiled Jake's mom.

5

At the big swimming pool,
Jake got into the water.
He loved swimming.

Max did not want to get in
at first.
He sat with his feet in the water
and looked at Jake.

Jake was swimming
up and down the pool.
He kicked his feet
and made big splashes.

Jake swam over to Max.
"I can't run very fast," he said,
"but I can swim fast."

"Yes," said Max.

"You are good at swimming."

"Put your hands on here,"
 said Jake,

"and kick your legs like this."

Grandpa and Jake's mom looked at the boys.

Jake and Max kicked the water. Max was having fun now.

"Swim over to me, Max," shouted Jake.

Max let go. He kicked his legs
and moved his hands.
He did not go down into the water.

"Look at me!" he shouted to Jake.
"I can swim now!"

Jake said,

"You helped me ride your bike,

and I helped you swim."